21st Century Skills Library

LIFE SKILLS BIOGRAPHIES

Yo-Yo Ma

D1709686

Annie Buckley

Cherry Lake Publishing
Ann Arbor, Michigan

Published in the United States of America by Cherry Lake Publishing
Ann Arbor, MI
www.cherrylakepublishing.com

Content Adviser: Paris-based author Richard Covington writes about the arts, culture, history and science for *Smithsonian*, the *International Herald Tribune*, *The Sunday Times of London*, and other publications.

Photo Credits: Cover and page 1, © Alex Grimm/Reuters/Corbis; page 5, © Pete Souza/ White House/Sygma/Corbis; pages 8 and 19, © Bettmann/Corbis; page 11, © Jean Louis Atlan/Sygma/Corbis; page 12, © Gail Mooney/Corbis; page 14, © Andrew Holbrooke/ Corbis; pages 23, 40, 41, and 42, © Reuters/Corbis; page 25, © Kim Kulish/Corbis; pages 28 and 30, AP Photo/Osamu Honda; page 31, AP Photo/Jennifer Gibson; page 32, © Joel Stettenheim/Corbis; page 34, © Kevin Lamarque/Reuters/Corbis; page 35, © Shawn Thew/epa/Corbis; page 36, © Steve Azzara/Corbis; page 37, © Lynn Goldsmith/Corbis; page 39, © Nancy Kaszerman/Zuma/Corbis

Library of Congress Cataloging-in-Publication Data
Buckley, Annie.
  Yo-Yo Ma / by Annie Buckley.
    p. cm. — (Life skills biographies)
  ISBN-13: 978-1-60279-077-3
  ISBN-10: 1-60279-077-9
  1. Ma, Yo-Yo 1955– —Juvenile literature. 2. Violoncellists—Biography—Juvenile literature.
I. Title. II. Series.
  ML3930.M11B83 2008
  787.4092—dc22
  [B]   2007006959

*Cherry Lake Publishing would like to acknowledge the work of
The Partnership for 21st Century Skills.
Please visit www.21stcenturyskills.org for more information.*

CONTENTS

INTRODUCTION

Yo-Yo Ma is one of the most famous classical musicians in the world. Considered by many to be the best cello player living today, he has played hundreds of concerts all around the world, recorded more than 50 CDs, and won numerous awards and much praise for his playing. His playful spirit, sense of humor, and interest in connecting with people around him have led him to explore new styles of music. His good nature and positive attitude are infectious, encouraging others to collaborate with him on new projects. And he is dedicated to helping aspiring young musicians and to sharing the music of diverse cultures with audiences around the world.

❧

CHAPTER ONE

AN EARLY START

Yo-Yo Ma was born on October 7, 1955, in Paris, France. The first son born to a very talented and musical family, Yo-Yo was a playful and lyrical baby. He could imitate the exact **tone** of any song he heard and also liked to dance and play jokes. Sometimes little Yo-Yo would crawl under the piano while his older sister, Yeou-Cheng, was playing and step on the pedals, interrupting her song. Soon enough, he got his own instrument and, like his sister, excelled at music.

Yo-Yo Ma entertains President and Mrs. Ronald Reagan and Japan's Emperor Akihito and Empress Michiko at the White House in 1987.

The cello has four strings and is usually played with a bow. It produces a rich, deep sound.

Though born in Paris, Yo-Yo and his sister were raised in New York City. Their parents were born and raised in China, and the couple first met at Nanjing University just before World War II (1939–1945). They met again years later in Paris.

Hiao-Tsiun Ma, Yo-Yo's father, was a violinist, composer, and music teacher. He was born and raised in Ningbo, a city south of Shanghai on China's coast. His mother, Marina Ma, was a singer and came from Hong Kong, an island off the coast of China.

Hiao-Tsiun studied music in Paris in the 1930s and then returned to China to teach at Nanjing University. But he didn't stay in China for long. The country was experiencing a change in leadership and great instability. In 1936, Hiao-Tsiun returned to Paris and continued his studies. He eventually earned a doctorate, the highest degree a person can receive, in musicology.

But Hiao-Tsiun's brief return to China was long enough to make a lasting impression on one of his students, a singer named Ya-Wen Lo. The young woman continued her studies after he left, but she did not forget about him. In 1949, when she was 26, Ya-Wen went to Paris, where Hiao-Tsiun's sister reintroduced her to Hiao-Tsiun.

On July 17, 1949, Hiao-Tsiun and Ya-Wen were married. At that time, she changed her name to Marina Ma. Their first child, Yeou-Cheng, was born in 1951, followed a few years later by Yo-Yo, whose name means "friendship" in Chinese.

CHOOSING THE CELLO

Yeou-Cheng and Yo-Yo's parents started teaching their children how to play instruments at a young age. Yeou-Cheng played piano and violin before she was three. When Yo-Yo was three, he also had lessons on the violin. But he wanted to play a different instrument—and a bigger one—than his sister. So when he was four, his father took him to the store to choose an instrument. Yo-Yo picked the cello, the biggest instrument he could find. Back home, the family stacked five telephone books for Yo-Yo to sit on, just so he could play his cello.

Yo-Yo Ma quickly advanced to playing music written by Johann Sebastian Bach (above) and other famous composers.

Even with their music lessons, the children still had time for play and schoolwork. Yo-Yo's father created a method of teaching his children that didn't require a lot of time. Each day, he taught them just one small part of a piece of music and only asked that they practice for 10 minutes. The key to this method was that, during short practices, the children fully concentrated on the music.

Learning in this way, Yo-Yo advanced quickly and was soon playing challenging music. Some of the first pieces he learned were written by Johann Sebastian Bach, a very famous composer who lived from 1685 to 1750. This music was part of six suites, or pieces, of music that Bach wrote specifically for the cello. They are called the Six Suites for Unaccompanied Cello.

Since Yo-Yo's father was a violinist, he decided to find his son a teacher who specialized in cello. When four-year-old Yo-Yo played three of the Bach suites from memory for his new teacher, Michelle Lepinte, she was very surprised. This was a huge accomplishment for such a young student. Lepinte was the first of many who would be impressed by Yo-Yo's talent. All of his teachers were thrilled to work with a student who was so motivated and learned so quickly.

When Yo-Yo was only five years old, he played his first public concert, at the University of Paris. He played some of the Bach suites, and the event was a big success. Shortly after the concert, the Ma family traveled to New York City to visit Hiao-Tsiun's brother and his family. While there, Yo-Yo's father was offered a job, and soon the Ma family moved to the city. In the United States, Yo-Yo's new teacher was Janos Scholtz, a well-known cellist. Yo-Yo's playing continued to improve with his new teacher.

Yo-Yo and Yeou-Cheng often played music and performed together, he on the cello and she on the piano. But their parents limited the number of

Learning & Innovation Skills

Hiao-Tsiun's method of teaching music emphasized staying focused on one thing at a time. This way, Yo-Yo learned to play complex music without being overwhelmed by the difficulty of the task. Even though Yo-Yo practiced many hours every day as he got older, he still referred to this technique throughout his life. In an interview with the *New Yorker* magazine, he explained, "When a problem is complex, you become tense, but when you break it down into basic components you can approach each element without stress. Then, when you put it together, you do something that seems externally complex, but you don't feel that way."

concerts they gave, believing that the children needed time for school and homework in addition to music. Nevertheless, Yo-Yo and his sister excelled at their instruments. Many people, including several famous musicians, began to notice them.

IMPRESSING PROFESSIONALS

When Yo-Yo was still very young, he gave a performance in the home of Pablo Casals, widely considered to be the best cellist at the time. After the performance, Casals introduced Yo-Yo to Leonard Bernstein, the conductor of the New York Philharmonic, a famous orchestra. Bernstein was also a famous composer and an important figure in music. He invited Yo-Yo and his sister to perform in a concert called the American Pageant of the Arts. This was a big honor. Yo-Yo was just seven and his sister 11 when they performed as a part of this event in Washington, D.C. President John F. Kennedy and his wife, Jacqueline, attended the concert, which was shown on national television. Yo-Yo and Yeou-Cheng were the youngest performers, but they received excellent reviews.

A famous violinist, Isaac Stern, had seen Yo-Yo perform in Paris and again in the United States. When Yo-Yo was nine, Stern introduced him to Leonard Rose, who would become Yo-Yo's teacher. Rose was a well-known cello player and taught at Juilliard, a **prestigious** school for the performing arts. Until he was 16, Yo-Yo studied with both Scholtz and Rose. He continued to study with Rose for many years after that. Rose was impressed that, at only 12, Yo-Yo had already mastered the most difficult material for cello. Yo-Yo counts Rose as an important influence in his life and career. When his teacher died in 1984, Yo-Yo grieved the loss of both a **mentor** and a friend.

FULL SCHEDULE

The year 1964 was a busy one for the young musician. He began attending classes at Juilliard on Saturdays. He made his first appearance as a soloist. He also performed with fellow Juilliard students at the world-famous Carnegie Hall in New York City. And he and Yeou-Cheng were guests on the *Johnny Carson Show*, a popular evening talk show.

Conductor Leonard Bernstein (above) was so impressed with Yo-Yo and his sister that he invited them to perform at a concert shown on national television.

Around this same time, in the fifth grade, Yo-Yo began to act out in school. He would often skip class and wander the halls. He later explained that he was struggling with his identity. Raised in Europe and the United States in a Chinese family, Yo-Yo may have felt confused about who he was

Yo-Yo Ma attended classes at the famous Juilliard School where talented young musicians, dancers, and actors study.

and how he should act. At home, he was quiet and obedient, which was the behavior typically expected of Chinese children. But in school, he noticed that children were encouraged to speak out and share their opinions.

The Ma family kept a tight schedule. The children each practiced music for 30 minutes before breakfast. After school, they had a snack, followed by another hour of music practice and two hours of homework. Yo-Yo was allowed a short time to watch television in the evening.

The family had fun together, too. In 1968, they traveled to California to visit Marina's sister, who lived in Berkeley. While there, Yo-Yo performed with the Little San Francisco Symphony Orchestra. He received excellent reviews in a local newspaper, the *San Francisco Chronicle*, and was invited back to perform with the San Francisco Orchestra in two years.

After the 1968 concert, invitations for Yo-Yo to perform poured into the Ma household. His career was off to an amazing start. But Yo-Yo was only 13 and, like most people his age, was still trying to figure out who he was and what he wanted.

21st Century Content

Throughout his life, Yo-Yo has explored other cultures and different ways of life. Experiencing two different cultures as a child eventually allowed him to understand multiple **perspectives** and, through music, to build bridges between Eastern cultures (such as those in China) and Western cultures (those in the United States and Europe). But as a young man, it was confusing for him. For Yo-Yo, balancing his two cultures led to questions that became a big part of his life's musical journey.

CHAPTER TWO

BALANCING ACT

Yo-Yo was still having difficulty in school. He often skipped class and was often inconsistent in his schoolwork. His parents decided to move him to a different school, the Professional Children's School, where he would be given the flexibility needed to continue to develop his career and attend school at the same time. But he continued to cut classes. His teachers decided that he must be bored, so they put him on an accelerated plan. In 1971, at the age of 15, Yo-Yo graduated from high school.

Yo-Yo Ma made his professional debut at Carnegie Hall in 1971.

That same year, he gave his first professional recital, also called his **debut**, at Carnegie Hall. In the audience that night was a young pianist named Emanuel Ax. Ax really enjoyed Yo-Yo's playing, and several years later, the two musicians teamed up to play together. Eventually, the Ax-Ma duo, as they were called, became very well known.

After high school, Yo-Yo wasn't sure what to do. He thought about going to Boston, where his sister was a college student at Radcliffe, and considered applying to nearby Harvard. But at 15, he may have felt that he was too young to live away from home. Maybe he wasn't quite ready to start a career as a professional musician. Instead, he spent the summer at a camp for young musicians, Meadowmount.

Meadowmount is located in the mountains in northern New York. The seven weeks Yo-Yo was there were his first away from his family. He still struggled to make sense of his Chinese heritage, French childhood, and American upbringing. It seems that he was still unsure about what he wanted to do with his life. Accounts of the young musician's life at this time show that, like many teenagers, he expressed his feelings through reckless behavior and pranks. But the emotions he felt also found their way into his music, and he began to play the cello with more feeling during this time.

When he returned to New York City, he continued to struggle. Yo-Yo enrolled at Columbia University and took classes at Juilliard. He also continued to study with Leonard Rose, a very **perceptive** teacher who gave his young student room to explore his own path and try different ways of playing. But Yo-Yo was still acting out. He left college without telling

Yo-Yo Ma met his wife, Jill, at a summer music program in 1972.

his parents. When they learned of his troubles and rebellious actions, they were both saddened and ashamed, but they believed in their son and helped him.

It was a difficult year. But at the end of it, Yo-Yo was invited to attend the 1972 summer program for talented musicians called the Marlboro Music School and Festival. That summer, he learned to play chamber music, a form of classical music written for small groups of players. He enjoyed playing this way, and throughout his career, he has included chamber music in his **repertoire**. At Marlboro, he studied with the world-famous cellist Pablo Casals, for whom he had performed at a young age, and was very inspired by him. At the end of the summer, Yo-Yo had decided what he wanted to do with his life: he wanted to be a professional musician.

That same summer, Yo-Yo met a young woman named Jill Horner. They forged a close friendship, and he liked the way she listened to him and seemed interested in what he had to say. The two remained close for many years and eventually married. But at that time, they were both young, so for the next few years they wrote letters and saw each other in the summers.

When Yo-Yo returned from that first summer at Marlboro, he decided he was ready for college. In 1972, he entered Harvard University in Cambridge, Massachusetts. But during his freshman year, he played so many concerts that his grades suffered. So after the first year, he talked with his father, who helped him make a plan. For the rest of his time at Harvard, he only played out-of-town concerts once a month. However, he continued to perform all over Boston and at school; he played everywhere he could, including the dorm room hallways.

Yo-Yo spent more than one summer at Marlboro, and he has said that the friends and mentors he met there were a huge influence on him. Having the opportunity to collaborate and learn from other musicians helped him find his own place as a musician. Cellist Pablo Casals was especially inspiring. Yo-Yo later said, "To see someone like Casals stand up in front of the orchestra and scream at the top of his voice was **catalytic**. I thought that if [he] can feel that strongly about music at 94 then I can stick with this for the next 50 years."

In college, students choose a major, an area to focus on in their studies. Yo-Yo Ma had already been studying and playing music since he was four years old. So while he took some music classes at Harvard, he chose to major in humanities, studies concerned mainly with human culture. He took classes in history, **anthropology**, German, and art. One of his favorite classes was an anthropology class taught by Professor Irven DeVore. In this class, he learned about a group of people in the Kalahari Desert in Africa called the San. Ma has said that this class changed his life because it helped him to see things from an entirely new point of view.

The music classes that Ma took at Harvard were mostly in a subject called music theory, which is a field of study that concentrates on analyzing how music is written. He wasn't interested in this at first and worried that too much analysis would hurt his instinct for simply playing the music. Once he learned more about it, though, he grew to enjoy it. These classes helped him to appreciate all the elements of a composition and gave him great respect for the composers who write the music he plays. He did take one class in which he performed. In this class, he studied chamber music with the well-known composer and pianist Leon Kirchner. Ma formed a trio with two classmates, violinist Lynn Chang and pianist Richard Kogan.

In 1976, Ma graduated from college. He had earned a degree, opened his mind to different perspectives, and made new friends. Now he was ready to set out on his path as a professional musician.

CHAPTER THREE

A RISING STAR

Yo-Yo Ma graduated from college in 1976 and began his full-time career as a musician.

Yo-Yo Ma played many concerts before and during college, but after graduating from Harvard, he began to play music full time. The first year, he was so excited by all the invitations to play that he traveled all over the world performing. He received many great reviews from music critics and audiences.

Around this time, he made a big step in his personal life as well. He

Yo-Yo Ma often addresses audiences during a performance. As he has said, "When I give a concert, I like to think that I'm welcoming someone into my home. I've lived with music for a long time; it's an old friend and I want to say, 'Let's all participate.'"

Ma's goal as a musician is to communicate with his audience, to welcome them into the music, as he says. While performing, he hopes to connect with listeners and to help them hear the meaning inside the music. This, together with his excellent playing, his generosity and skill as a teacher, and his consistent willingness to experiment, are the **hallmarks** of his **illustrious** career.

proposed to his longtime girlfriend, Jill Horner. They had been together for almost five years, and she said yes. Ma's parents had hoped he would marry a Chinese woman. But Ma made up his own mind and chose to marry the woman he loved. He was willing to do what was right for him even if it did not meet with his parents' approval. His parents soon came to accept Jill as part of the family. Throughout his marriage, Ma has said, his relationship with Jill has continued to be a source of love and support.

In 1978, Ma won an important award called the Avery Fisher Prize, which is given to outstanding classical musicians in the United States. After winning the award, he received more invitations than ever to perform. During the early years of his professional career, he traveled almost constantly. He played as many as 125 concerts a year. His fall and spring seasons were spent performing around the world, and during the summers, he taught music at festivals and camps like those he had attended as a young man.

Ma proved to be an excellent teacher, always finding the positive aspects in a student's playing before making suggestions about how to improve. For his performances, Ma continued to use his father's method of focusing intently on one part at a time. Each concert season, he chose two or three compositions to focus on and play. He played music written long ago by composers such as Bach and Haydn, but he learned some contemporary pieces each season, too. Ma is a big supporter of contemporary music and music from many cultures and time periods.

Ma had begun playing with Emanuel Ax in 1975 and continued to play several concerts with him each year. In 1980, Ma played with the trio he had formed at Harvard with Lynn Chang and Richard Kogan. Around this time, Ma was faced with a serious threat to his health and career. He had a severe case of scoliosis (his spine was excessively curved) and needed to undergo an operation. If the surgery was not successful, he might not have been able to play the cello afterward. But the surgery was a success.

KEEPING HIMSELF CHALLENGED

In addition to his busy concert schedule, Yo-Yo Ma continued to experiment with playing different

Life & Career Skills

Facing a surgery that could potentially change his life did not **deter** Yo-Yo Ma. Throughout, he remained **optimistic** and flexible. Rather than focusing on the problem, he thought about what he would do if he couldn't play music anymore and decided that he would be prepared to do something else if necessary. After the surgery, he wore a cast on his upper body for six months. But he continued to play cello and even gave one concert wearing his cast. Being flexible enough to see the possibilities in a challenging situation helped Yo-Yo Ma in his work and his life. The ability to see the positive sides of any situation, and to find alternative solutions to problems, is helpful on the road to happiness and success.

kinds of music and to pose new challenges for himself. In 1981, he decided to adapt music originally written for the violin by an Italian composer named Niccolò Paganini to fit the cello. The pieces he chose were some of the most difficult ever written for the violin. Adapting them for cello, as well as playing them, required a lot of hard work. When Ma finished, he gave a concert debuting this new music. He was very nervous beforehand, but the performance was a big success. He later said he was glad to have taken on this difficult task and completed it.

Not too long afterward, he took on more new challenges. For the first time, he made a recording of the Bach suites that he had learned as a child. And he became a father. Yo-Yo and Jill's first child, Nicholas, was born in 1983. Their second, Emily, was born two years later, in 1985. Ma continued to travel and perform, but he was concerned about spending enough time with his family. He consulted with the famous violinist Itzhak Perlman. On Perlman's recommendation, Ma made more time for family by setting aside the month of July to spend with them instead of playing concerts.

*Violinist Itzhak Perlman (left) gave Yo-Yo Ma (right) advice
that helped him balance his career and family life.*

His recording of the suites proved to be as popular as his performances, and it earned Yo-Yo Ma his first Grammy Award in 1984. (He has since won many more Grammys.) The Bach suites continue to hold a special place in his work and life. At his father's request, Ma played them for his father before he died in 1991. And in the 1990s, he decided to make a

Life & Career Skills

After his first child was born, Yo-Yo Ma sat down and made a list of priorities. He knew that as a father he would have less time for music, and he wanted all his time to be well spent. He decided that every concert he gave, no matter the size, would be something special and he would always try his best. He also decided that he would give up playing and performing if he was too overwhelmed by it or if he lost his enthusiasm and passion for music. Setting goals and priorities helped him to make decisions about which concerts to accept. Recognizing what is most important to achieve often brings focus.

film interpreting the Bach suites through the eyes of different artists. In *Inspired by Bach,* the cellist invited well-known creative people from different fields, such as ice dancers and a garden designer, to interpret the suites. Ma appeared in the film as well. When it aired in 1997, it received uneven praise, but he was still happy to have done it.

BEYOND CLASSICAL MUSIC

While rising to fame, Ma continually experimented with new forms. Over the 1980s and 1990s, he performed and recorded jazz music and bluegrass. He played contemporary electronic music and then remade his cello to play in an old style from hundreds of years ago. He has played on soundtracks for films such as *Crouching Tiger, Hidden Dragon* and *Seven Years in Tibet,* and on children's television shows such as *Mister Rogers' Neighborhood* and *Arthur.*

By taking his music and ideas outside the concert hall, he has helped to introduce classical music—traditionally seen as something only for an educated few—to a wider audience. And his love of music, his adventurous spirit, and his curious, friendly style are infectious. Yet, despite his wildly

Yo-Yo Ma performed with rock musician Sting at the opening ceremonies for the 2002 Winter Olympics.

Not all of Yo-Yo Ma's experiments receive the same **acclaim** as his classical cello playing, but he isn't afraid to try them anyway. Ma made a jazz recording with violinist Stephane Grappelli that wasn't very popular. But a few years later, his efforts to learn the methods of jazz paid off when he performed onstage with jazz singer Bobby McFerrin and was asked to improvise, or make something up, as he went along. Having played jazz before, Ma was familiar with this style of playing. Even though he said he was shaking, he tried it onstage. Doing things he wanted to do but was nervous about, or that people said he couldn't do, has kept Ma's career fun. His listeners have benefited as well.

successful career, Ma refers to himself as "just a performing musician." Sometimes he sits in with the orchestra after he finishes his solo performing their pieces along with them, which is unusual. But he considers playing with the orchestra an honor. It's just one more way Ma brings the nontraditional to the traditional.

CHAPTER FOUR

BRIDGING EAST AND WEST

*These sand dunes are located in the Kalahari Desert. Yo-Yo Ma flew
to the Kalahari to learn about the life and culture of the San.*

In 1993, Yo-Yo Ma boarded a plane and flew across the world yet again,
only this time it was not for a concert. He traveled, together with a
translator and a film crew, to the Kalahari Desert in Africa. His goal was
to meet members of the San, the group he first learned about at Harvard.
They live in a hunting and gathering society, unlike modern cities, and
speak an unfamiliar language. The San's life and culture fascinated Ma,
and he had not forgotten about them. Finally, with the help of his former
professor Irven DeVore, Ma was going to experience the culture firsthand.

The trip proved to be a turning point in Ma's life and career. While he had always explored different forms of music, they had been primarily types of music from the West, which means from Europe or North America. In Africa, he encountered something completely different. He was moved by the experience of playing music for and with the San. He enjoyed communicating with them and felt afterward that the role of a musician is to help to communicate cultural history, as well as to create new ideas and forms.

The San way of life fascinated Yo-Yo Ma and he enjoyed learning about their music and other aspects of their culture.

Yo-Yo Ma (second from left) plays with musicians Colin Jacobsen (far left) and Joseph Gramley (middle)from the United States and Chinese musicians Wu Tong (second from right) and Wu Man (far right) during a 2002 Silk Road Ensemble concert.

After this amazing journey, Ma decided to cut his performance schedule down to about 75 concerts a year. He wanted to make time for other projects that explore new ways of bringing music to people and how different cultures communicate through music. One of these projects was the film *Inspired by Bach;* another was an investigation of tango music in Argentina.

A few years after his trip to Africa, Yo-Yo Ma began a project that he would dedicate himself to for many years: the Silk Road Project, which he founded in 1998. Through it, Ma connects musicians from all over the East with those in the West. He is interested in what happens when people unfamiliar with each other come together to play music and what each can learn and share. The first performance and recording of this complex and exciting project was titled *When Strangers Meet*, released in 2002.

The Silk Road is an ancient trade route that connected the continent of Asia to the area around the Mediterranean Sea. People from different cultures met along this road. Traders on the Silk Road brought artworks, raw materials, and plants from one region to another. Ma was interested in what happened when they met, and what would happen today if musicians from different countries met and played music together.

In the project's first four years, Ma collaborated with a professor from Dartmouth College named Theodore Levin. Levin is an ethnomusicologist, which means he studies different cultures through learning about their music. Together, they compiled a list of composers from all over the East. A panel chose 16 of them, and each was **commissioned** to create a piece of music for the project. The composers came from the countries of Azerbaijan, Tajikistan, China,

In the introduction to a children's book titled *Caravan to America*, Yo-Yo Ma writes, "After twenty-five years of performing the cello in different parts of the world, I have learned how effectively music speaks to people everywhere, despite what at first might seem like very great cultural differences." Inspired by what he learned on his travels, he created a project that would allow musicians and audiences to hear and learn about music from around the globe.

Yo-Yo Ma performs with two other members of the Silk
Road Ensemble at Carnegie Hall in May 2002.

Mongolia, and Iran. The music they played was not Western music or
traditional classical music that Ma played in most of his concerts, but music
unique to each culture.

    While the composers were still developing their music for the project,
Ma composed his own music inspired by what he heard them play.
When he performed this new music in concerts, critics were worried that
audiences wouldn't appreciate or understand it because it was different

from what they were used to hearing Ma play. But audiences enjoyed it and gave him standing **ovations**, just as they did when he played more traditional music for the cello. His new compositions were educating people about different kinds of music and helping them to see a new

Yo-Yo Ma displays a kamancheh, *an ancient Persian spiked fiddle.*

The twin towers of the World Trade Center once dominated the skyline of New York City. The tragic events of September 11, 2001, when terrorists destroyed the towers, caused the Silk Road Ensemble to postpone its visit to Central Asia.

perspective. But these concerts were only the beginning.

In 2000, the Silk Road musicians and composers were ready to practice for their first performance. Ma arranged a session for the musicians to practice and get to know each other. Levin and Ma also invited Western musicians to participate, and Ma learned a new instrument, the *morin khur*. It has only two strings and comes from Mongolia. The top of the instrument has a carving of a horse's head. Yo-Yo Ma's family name is related to the Chinese word for horse, so he chose this instrument partly to reflect his family history.

Ma continued to perform all over the world, and he appeared in an episode of the popular television show *The West Wing*. Meanwhile, the Silk Road Project grew to include the works of composers from more countries, including Japan, India, Korea, and Turkey. By 2001, the Silk Road Ensemble was ready to perform. Ma and Levin scheduled a tour that included many countries and featured workshops and festivals at each stop. The tour began in Germany, and audiences loved it.

But before the Silk Road Ensemble could travel to its next destination in Central Asia, tragedy struck in the United States. On September 11, 2001, nearly 3,000 people were killed when terrorists flew two planes into the World Trade Center in New York City, one into the Pentagon in Washington D.C., and one into a field in Pennsylvania. These events caused concern for the safety of air travel, so the Silk Road Ensemble's visit to Central Asia was postponed.

After September 11, Yo-Yo Ma was faced with a decision. Should he continue the world tour of the Silk Road Ensemble, with its message of appreciating diversity and artistic expression, or should he cancel it in the interest of safety? The world was in a fearful and insecure state. Yo-Yo Ma decided to continue the tour, despite the uncertain times. He felt that the music could be a way for people to come together, so rather than cancel the tour, the ensemble traveled to Washington, D.C., then continued on to Japan, Europe, and back to the United States.

The tour to Central Asia was rescheduled for 2003, and the Silk Road

Yo-Yo Ma rehearses with a group of Iraqi musicians.

Ensemble performed and gave classes in Kazakhstan, Kyrgyzstan, and Tajikistan. The Silk Road Project continues to inspire audiences and other musicians. By facilitating and participating in this project, Yo-Yo Ma has brought together people from different cultures, sparking countless connections among them. His belief in the power of music has allowed him to bridge the boundaries of languages and ideas, to educate people about different ways of creating music, and to uplift audiences with a wonderful and unique selection of music.

CHAPTER FIVE

MUSIC FOR ALL

Yo-Yo Ma strives to bring interesting and beautiful music to people everywhere. From a very young age, he has accomplished this goal through hard work, passion for music, and curiosity about people and cultures from all over the world. Internationally recognized for his excellent and innovative playing, he continues to create a brilliant legacy of music, creativity, and education.

Yo-Yo-Ma speaks with the conductor at a rehearsal of the combined U.S. and Iraqi National Symphony Orchestras.

Yo-Yo Ma arrives at the Grammy Awards in 2003. Ma has won many Grammy Awards for his music.

Ma is most famous for his flawless performances, technical **virtuosity**, and expressive playing of more traditional orchestral pieces. He has played the Bach suites for the cello throughout his life, in addition to music by other famous composers such as Brahms, Schubert, and Prokofiev. Because of his talent and years of hard work and practice, Ma reached the highest level possible on his instrument.

But exceptional technical playing was not enough for him. Ma has always wanted to reach beyond the notes and into the meaning or spirit of the music. He wants the music to connect to people, to move them. This desire is present in each of his performances and makes him not just a great musician, but the world-famous one he is today.

Ma's creative explorations—such as playing jazz, mixing classical and tango, remaking his cello to play in the style of the 1700s, and integrating Eastern music with Western music—have left a trail of new and exciting ideas. Musicians the world over are influenced and inspired by Ma's work. Young musicians who see him trying new ways of playing and mixing styles are inspired to do the same.

As a recording artist, Yo-Yo Ma has created an equally

Jazz musician Bobby McFerrin is just one of the many artists that Yo-Yo Ma has collaborated with.

Yo-Yo Ma wants audiences to connect with his music and to recognize the meaning in the music. His goal as a musician is clear, and by knowing what is important to him, he is able to approach various kinds of music and audiences all over the world and still achieve his goal. Each time, he finds a way to reach out to audiences.

It might take time to understand exactly what is important to you or what you want to communicate to others. Maybe you want to be a good listener or help people or explore new ideas. But once you know what you want, you can focus on working toward these goals, regardless of the activity.

impressive legacy. In the course of his career, he has recorded more than 50 albums and won 15 Grammy Awards. Because of the early success of his recordings, Sony Music, a large recording company, offered him an exclusive contract.

Despite his talent and fame, Ma is humble and generous. He does not think of himself as a star but as one of the many performing musicians. He has a deep respect for composers as well as for the other musicians with whom he performs. Ma has continually offered his time to help teach young musicians, spending many summers at festivals and camps like the ones he had attended when he was young. He is always able to find something special in each student's playing and helps them reach a higher level. The 1989 documentary film, *Yo-Yo Ma: A Month at Tanglewood,* focuses on his work as a teacher. He also made a series of educational tapes with trumpet player Wynton Marsalis.

In addition to his many professional accomplishments, Ma is a committed husband and father. He and Jill live in Boston, Massachusetts, where they raised their two children. In the early days of their marriage, when their

Yo-Yo Ma promotes his 2004 album Vivaldi's Cello.

children were growing up, Ma adjusted his touring schedule so he could spend more time with his family. He credits them with his ability to form powerful connections with his audiences. He says, "Their love allows me to really care about people and then to be able to communicate feelings, ideas and ideals."

The skills and **attributes** that have helped Yo-Yo Ma to be a great musician can be applied to any area of life. At an early age, he learned the value of concentration. The ability to focus on one thing at a time can be applied to any endeavor.

For example, if you have a big test coming up, you can break the information down into pieces. Learn each one, focusing completely on one part at a time, and in the end you will be prepared. This is a more successful way to study than trying to learn everything a few hours before the test. This technique can be applied to how we view each day, too. It is valuable to plan ahead and set goals, but focusing on what is in front of you, be it work or play, is also worthwhile and can make life fuller and more interesting.

Yo-Yo Ma has developed his ability to concentrate on one thing at a time.

Yo-Yo Ma has also learned to set goals and priorities. He knew he couldn't do exceedingly well in every class at Harvard while touring extensively, so he made it a priority to be in school and limited his out-of-town concerts. However, performing locally still took up a lot of time. So Ma decided to choose one class each semester in which he would excel. For the other classes, he did the best he could, but he didn't worry about learning everything or achieving perfect

Yo-Yo Ma's playing appears effortless because of the countless hours he spends practicing. By mastering each piece, he can concentrate on making the music come alive when he plays for an audience.

Yo-Yo Ma (left) shares a laugh with pianist Emanuel Ax (center) as actor Peter Ustinov (right) delivers a comic tribute to famous violinist Isaac Stern.

scores. In this way, he was able to feel successful about his results, even if they were not what others might have expected of him.

In his performing career, Ma set a goal of making each concert special. This way, before getting on the stage—whether he is nervous, excited, or tired—he always remembers that he wants to make the music come alive for his audience, so he focuses on that. Having priorities and goals makes it easier to do your best and to make choices.

Ma made a decision as a young man to explore what was important to him. Most of his ideas and explorations have been hugely successful, but not all. Doing what he believes in, however, Ma remains true to his vision as an artist and has been able to enjoy the path to his success. The point is not that the result was positive, but that he was courageous enough to discover what was important or interesting or curious, and give it a try. Though some people thought classical music did not belong with jazz, he mixed them anyway. When others thought that blending Eastern and Western sounds would not be successful, he still continued with the Silk Road Project.

As with any artist, this story is not complete without the art. Yo-Yo Ma's life and work are inspiring to read about, but to truly appreciate them, you must turn to his music. Fortunately, he plays widely and has recorded many albums that feature his various interests. Listen and let the music tell you his story!

TIMELINE

1955 Yo-Yo Ma is born in Paris, France, on October 7.

1959 Yo-Yo receives his first cello at age four.

1960 Yo-Yo performs his first concert at the University of Paris.

1962 Ma family moves to New York City.

1964 Yo-Yo begins studying with Leonard Rose; Yo-Yo begins taking classes at Juilliard.

1968 Yo-Yo receives rave reviews for his performance with the Little San Francisco Symphony Orchestra.

1971 Yo-Yo has his professional debut at New York's Carnegie Hall.

1972 Yo-Yo attends the Marlboro Music School and Festival; he meets Jill Horner; he enters Harvard University.

1976 Ma graduates from Harvard University with a bachelor's degree in humanities.

1978 Ma marries Jill Horner; he receives the Avery Fisher Prize.

1980 Ma undergoes a successful operation to correct his scoliosis.

1983 Ma's first child, Nicholas, is born.

1984 Ma receives his first Grammy Award.

1985 Ma's second child, Emily, is born; Ma wins two Grammys.

1986 Ma wins a Grammy Award for Best Chamber Music Performance for a recording made with Emanuel Ax.

1991 Ma receives an honorary doctorate from Harvard University; his father dies.

1992 Ma releases a hit recording with vocalist Bobby McFerrin.

1993 Ma travels to the Kalahari Desert to meet the San.

1998 *Inspired by Bach* airs on BBC; Ma founds the Silk Road Project.

2000 Ma receives his 14th Grammy Award.

2001 The Silk Road Project begins its first tour.

2002 The first Silk Road Ensemble recording, *When Strangers Meet*, is released.

2005 Ma collaborates with John Williams and Itzhak Perlman for the soundtrack to *Memoirs of a Geisha*

2007 Ma releases *Appassionato*, a recording billed as his musical autobiography

GLOSSARY

acclaim (uh-KLAYM) praise or publicity that is very positive and enthusiastic

anthropology (an-thruh-POL-uh-jee) the study of the beliefs and ways of life of different people around the world

attributes (AT-ruh-byoots) specific qualities or characteristics

catalytic (ka-tuh-LIH-tik) causing a reaction or something to happen

commissioned (kuh-MISH-uhnd) given money to create something original

debut (day-BYOO) a first public appearance, usually related to a performance or presentation

deter (dih-TURR) to discourage or prevent from action

hallmarks (HAWL-markss) features that distinguish something from others

illustrious (ih-LUHS-tree-uhs) very famous and deserving of renown

mentor (MEN-tor) a person who provides advice and support, usually to someone less experienced

optimistic (op-tuh-MISS-tik) expecting the best possible outcome

ovations (oh-VAY-shuhnz) enthusiastic applause from a crowd or a group

perceptive (pur-SEP-tiv) having the ability to understand people or situations

perspectives (pur-SPEK-tivz) points of view; the places from which people observe or perceive

prestigious (preh-STEE-juhss) very important; having a distinguished reputation

repertoire (REP-ur-twar) the group of musical material that a player knows and can perform

tone (tohn) a sound or a particular quality of sound

virtuosity (vur-choo-AH-sih-tee) great skill or technique

FOR MORE INFORMATION

Books

Chippendale, Lisa A. *Yo-Yo Ma: A Cello Superstar Brings Music to the World.* Berkeley Heights, NJ: Enslow Publishers, 2004.

Gan, Geraldine. *Lives of Notable Asian Americans.* New York: Chelsea House Publishers, 1995.

Major, John S., and Betty Belanus. *Caravan to America: Living Arts of the Silk Road.* Chicago: Cricket Books, 2002.

Web Sites

Yo-Yo Ma's Official Web Site

www.yo-yoma.com
For music, photos, and an interview

Silk Road Project

www.silkroadproject.org
Includes updates on tours, CDs, and new music

On the Silk Road with Yo-Yo Ma

www.npr.org/programs/wesat/features/2002/may/yoyo
Features an interview with Yo-Yo Ma on National Public Radio

INDEX

ABOUT THE AUTHOR

Annie Buckley is a writer, artist, and teacher. She has written books for kids about many topics such as yoga, creative writing, and heroic girls. She also writes about art and culture for magazines. She was thrilled to research and write about the life and work of Yo-Yo Ma. In addition to his amazing dedication to his art, she was inspired by Ma's courage to explore different types of music and his efforts to bridge Eastern and Western music through the Silk Road Project. She has practiced yoga and meditation for many years and enjoys the possibilities that come from blending the wisdom and arts of East and West.